CITIES OF THE DEAD

Cities of the Dead

Historic New Orleans Cemeteries

Photography by
CARL D. ROBINSON, M.D.

Text by
JENNIE N. ROBINSON, APRN

Lafayette, Louisiana

On the Cover – New Orleans cemeteries are sometimes referred to as "cities of the dead," in part because above-ground graves lined up neatly in rows – such as these in Lafayette Cemetery 1 – bear a resemblance to a residential neighborhood. They are like "cities," too, because some of them cover huge amounts of land; two of the largest ones take up about 150 acres each.

Copyright © 2020 by Dr. Carl D. Robinson and Jennie N. Robinson

All rights reserved, including the right to reproduce this book or portions thereof in any form whatsoever. For information, contact Acadian House Publishing, P.O. Box 52247, Lafayette, Louisiana 70505, or via e-mail: info@acadianhouse.com.

Library of Congress Control Number: 2019953093

ISBN 10: 0-9995884-0-0
ISBN 13: 978-0-9995884-0-6

- Published by Acadian House Publishing, Lafayette, Louisiana
  (Trent Angers and Madison Louviere, co-editors)
- Design and pre-press production by Allison Nassans
- Printed by Bang Printing, Brainerd, Minnesota

*For Nellie Williams
(Jennie's mother and Carl's mother-in-law),
who moved from her beloved New Orleans
to Arizona after Hurricane Katrina.*

*When asked how she's doing
she likes to say,
"I'm still above ground."*

Contents

Preface . . . . *viii*
1. St. Louis Cemetery 1 12
2. St. Louis Cemetery 2 20
3. Lafayette Cemetery 1 & 2 30
4. Cypress Grove Cemetery 36
5. Dispersed of Judah 42
6. Greenwood Cemetery 48
7. St. Louis Cemetery 3 54
8. Hebrew Rest Cemetery 60
9. Masonic Cemetery 66
10. Metairie/Lake Lawn Cemetery 72
11. St. Roch Cemetery 90
    In Memoriam: The New Orleans Katrina Memorial . . 98
    Appendix 1: Map locating New Orleans cemeteries 100
    Appendix 2: Types of burial vaults 102
    Appendix 3: Timeline: New Orleans history 103
    Sources 104
    Index 105
    About the Author and the Photographer 109

Preface

New Orleans history reflected in its cemeteries

New Orleans is a place of history and mystery, and nowhere is this more evident than in the above-ground cemeteries that are scattered around the city.

The oldest tombs are found in St. Louis Cemetery 1, and the most opulent are in Metairie/Lake Lawn Cemetery. There is a towering monument to the city's firefighters in Greenwood Cemetery, and other monuments memorializing Confederate soldiers who died in the Civil War can be found in both Greenwood and Metairie/Lake Lawn.

Eleven cemeteries are featured in *Cities of the Dead*. The graves and monuments that are pictured are, generally speaking, the historically significant, the aesthetically beautiful, and the simply heartrending.

But these graveyards also have their fair share of the curious, the off-beat, the one-of-a-kind. Not the least of these is the tomb of the legendary Voodoo priestess Marie Laveau. Then there is the tomb of the vampire Lestat, a fictional character in author Anne Rice's bestselling novel, *Interview With The Vampire*. (Actually, this cast iron tomb, imported from Germany sometime in the mid-1800s, holds the remains of some of the Karstendiek Family.) One other tomb in a league of its own, and as yet unoccupied, is a 9-foot-high, pyramid-shaped structure owned by Hollywood actor Nicolas Cage, who intends to be buried in The City That Care Forgot.

Among the historically significant are the graves of Jacques Philippe Villere, the second governor of Louisiana; the tomb of Earnest "Dutch" Morial, first black mayor of New Orleans; and the final resting places for countless men who died in every war since the American Revolution. Also of note are the graves of both Homer Plessy and Judge John H. Ferguson, who were principals in the 1896 landmark U.S. Supreme Court case, Plessy vs. Ferguson, that upheld the constitutionality of the "separate but equal" doctrine of racial segregation; that law would be nullified some 60 years later.

Some of the better known business and civic

leaders of the city found their final resting places in local cemeteries. These include Tom Benson, long-time owner of the New Orleans Saints NFL franchise; Al Copeland, founder of Popeye's Fried Chicken; Fabacher Family members who founded Jackson Brewery, maker of the locally famous JAX beer; Besthoff Family members who started the once-flourishing Katz & Besthoff pharmacy chain; and Delgado Family members who left a fortune for Delgado Museum, Charity Hospital and Delgado Community College.

Tombs that are exceptionally beautiful and/or masterfully designed are plentiful. A few examples are the J.M. Pelton Family tomb in Greenwood that features a cast iron image of an angel comforting a bereaved woman; the Levi Family tomb topped by an exquisite life-size winged angel, in Hebrew Rest; and the ornate mausoleum of Capt. Salvatore Pizzati with its medieval turrets and Byzantine columns, in Metairie/Lake Lawn.

Just the sight of certain statues topping some tombs are positively heartrending, not the least of which is that of a mother holding the lifeless body of her child. The inscription alone on one communal tomb evokes emotions of pity: Society for the Relief of Destitute Orphan Boys.

While visually impressive tombs are plentiful in New Orleans, so are the simpler communal graves of members of various fraternal and benevolent associations. They tell a story of people banning together to care for one another in life and in death. Among the many are the Firemen's Charitable Assn., Italian Mutual Benevolent Society, the Chinese Soon On Tong Assn., Red River Pilots Assn. and Dante Masonic Lodge.

Another memorable group in this category is the *Dieu Nous Protégé* Society (God Protect Us Society), a benevolent association of free people of color who, in antebellum times, raised money to buy the freedom of slaves and later helped to pay for their medical bills and funerals.

A good number of communal tombs of religious congregations testify to the predominance of Roman Catholicism in New Orleans during much of its history. These include graves of Sisters of the Holy Family, Servants of Mary, and Sisters of St. Joseph.

Indeed, much of the rich history of New Orleans can be gleaned from her cemeteries.

– Trent Angers,
Editor

A scene from Metairie/Lake Lawn Cemetery

Cities of the Dead

CHAPTER 1

St. Louis Cemetery 1
(425 Basin Street at St. Louis Street)

Saint Louis Cemetery 1, the oldest extant and most historically significant cemetery in New Orleans, was established by a royal decree of Spain on August 17, 1789, and is owned today by New Orleans Catholic Cemeteries.

The vast majority of the tombs are above ground and are made from locally produced soft bricks covered in plaster. The cemetery was arranged with little regard for order, without a master plan. Today the tombs of many shapes are leaning this way and that due to natural subsidence with the passage of time.

St. Louis Cemetery 1 was begun in response to the overcrowding of St. Peter Street Cemetery. This overcrowding was due

---

Marie Laveau, 'Voodoo Queen' (1794-1881)
Practitioners of Voodoo believe the spirit of "the Voodoo Queen" is alive and present and can be contacted through certain rituals conducted around her tomb. Voodoo is a mutation of a West African religion that mixes in elements of Caribbean spiritualism and Roman Catholicism. Laveau, who was actually a devout Catholic, was a free woman of color, born to a wealthy French planter.

to the rapid growth of the population of New Orleans.

Several veterans of the Battle of New Orleans are buried here. So is Jean Étienne de Boré (1741–1820), the first mayor of New Orleans and first to produce granulated sugar on a commercial scale.

Here one will also find the tombs of Homer Plessy (1862–1925) and Marie Laveau (1794–1881), the Voodoo priestess.

St. Louis Cemetery 1 is crowded, like New Orleans itself. To save land, the above-ground tombs have been used over and over again. (A local custom has it that the minimum amount of time a casket must remain entombed is "a year and a day" – the generally accepted time needed for a corpse to decompose.)

Dieu Nous Protégé Society tomb (God Protect Us Society)

This tomb for free people of color contains 20 vaults and dates back to 1844. An African-American benevolent association, Dieu Nous Protégé, at first raised money to buy slaves' freedom and later helped to pay for their medical bills and funerals.

Homer Plessy tomb (1862-1925)

Plessy was the plaintiff in the 1896 landmark U.S. Supreme Court case, Plessy vs. Ferguson, that upheld the constitutionality of racial segregation laws for public facilities–so long as they were "separate but equal." Ferguson was the local judge who kept Plessy, a black man, in jail for sitting in the white section of a train. Plessy's attorney argued the judge's actions violated Plessy's 14th Amendment rights (equal protection under the law), but he lost the case.

Some 58 years later, in 1954, the separate-but-equal doctrine was rejected in the Supreme Court case of Brown vs. Board of Education (of Topeka, Kansas) as the justices ruled unanimously that racial segregation of children in public schools is unconstitutional.

Nicolas Cage tomb ▶

This pyramid-shaped tomb was built for and is owned by Hollywood actor Nicolas Cage. (Apparently, he fancied the idea of being buried in an historic New Orleans cemetery, when the time comes.) The huge, 9-foot-high tomb bears the motto, Omnia Ab Uno, which is Latin for "Everything from one." The phrase and an image of a pyramid were used in the Disney film National Treasure, in which Cage played a treasure hunter.

◀ Myra Clark Gaines (1806-1885)

Here lies the remains of the "illegitimate" daughter of multi-millionaire Daniel Clark, a New Orleans businessman and politician. Myra embarked on and finally won the longest civil lawsuit in U.S. history, lasting nearly 60 years, from 1834 to 1891. Unfortunately for her, she died before the case was resolved; her heirs received a settlement of nearly $1 million–six years after Myra's death. Myra had sued for the inheritance to which she felt entitled; the suit involved her father's will and the "forced heirship" laws.

Cities of the Dead

Italian Mutual Benevolent Society tomb

The tallest structure in the cemetery, this marble tomb was built in 1857 in a Baroque circular design with 24 vaults. It is surrounded by three female figures: one on top holding a cross representing "Faith" (see detail above), one representing "Italia," and the other with two children representing "Charity."

The Protestant Section

Set aside in 1805 near the rear of the cemetery, this section is noticeably different from other parts that feature above-ground graves. Originally, it was referred to by French Catholics as "The Cemetery of the Heretics" – a term applied to Christians who didn't subscribe to the totality of Catholic doctrine. Colonial Louisiana was predominantly Roman Catholic, but thousands of Protestants came to the region soon after the Louisiana Purchase of 1803.

St. Louis Cathedral

Founded in 1720, St. Louis Cathedral was used extensively for funeral-related services throughout its first century of operation. However, circa 1820-25, church officials stopped allowing the bodies of yellow fever victims to be brought into the cathedral because of the very real possibility of spreading the disease to its parishioners. Subsequently, in 1826, the Mortuary Chapel was built several blocks away to accommodate these funerals. (More about the yellow fever epidemics can be found on page 27.)

The Mortuary Chapel

The Mortuary Chapel of Saint Anthony was built in 1826 and is located on the corner of North Rampart and Conti streets, approximately one block southwest of St. Louis Cemetery 1 and 4 blocks from St. Louis Cemetery 2. It is the oldest church building in New Orleans.

It served as a funeral church when funerals at St. Louis Cathedral were no longer allowed due to fear of the spread of disease from so many dead bodies during the epidemics. It was used solely as a mortuary chapel until 1860. Today, it is called Our Lady of Guadalupe church and is still in service.

CHAPTER 2

St. Louis Cemetery 2

(300 N. Claiborne Ave.)

Francois Xavier Martin (1762-1846)

He is the author of the first history of Louisiana and was a noted jurist in his time. Martin is memorialized on this 27-foot granite obelisk, erected in 1847.

Saint Louis Cemetery 2 was established in response to a city-wide fear of contagion from a series of epidemics, particularly yellow fever.

Consecrated in August of 1823, it is the second-oldest extant cemetery in New Orleans. It is located four blocks from Saint Louis Cemetery 1, and they are separated by what was once the area of town known as Storyville, the "Red Light District." It is bounded by Robertson Street, St. Louis Street, Iberville Street and Claiborne Avenue.

Noted for its abundance of fine ironwork, it abounds with Baroque, Gothic, and Egyptian Revival architecture. Many of the tombs were designed by noted architect J. N. B. de Pouilly, who was buried here in one of the wall vaults that define most of the outer edges of the cemetery.

Saint Louis Cemetery 2 reflects the racial

history of New Orleans. In 1824, Antoine Phillip LeRiche, a Paris-born architect-engineer, began building the cemetery, with 30 tombs for whites and 30 for blacks at $50 each. From early in its history the cemetery was divided into three distinct squares. Of these, the square between Iberville and Bienville streets contains tombs owned almost exclusively by African-Americans.

New Orleans was once referred to as "North America's most African city," having a strong West African presence from the beginning. The city had a widely known tradition of wealthy political men keeping mistresses of mixed races, many of whom are buried here.

Lanusse-McCarthy Family tomb

A large, sturdy Latin botonee cross stands above the ornate enclosure, which is the tallest in the cemetery.

22 Cities of the Dead

Dominique You
A native of Santo Domingo, he was an artilleryman in Napoleon's army. He later joined Jean Lafitte's militia and used his skill with operating cannons to give the American forces the advantage in the final conflict of the War of 1812.

Wall vaults that accommodate numerous burials can be found in cemeteries throughout New Orleans.

Sisters of the Holy Family

More than 200 of the sisters of this religious congregation of African-American teachers are buried in this cemetery. Founded in 1842, the congregation ministered to the dying, the sick and the elderly, and they taught catechism to slaves and free people of color. In the twentieth century the sisters educated descendants of slaves in New Orleans, Grand Coteau and Bellevue, Louisiana, as well as in other locales.

Mother Henriette Delille, Servant of God (1813-1862)

Founder of the Sisters of the Holy Family, Henriette Delille was a free woman of color in antebellum New Orleans. She was revered by those who knew of her good deeds and her faith-filled life. Her obituary noted:

"The crowd gathered for her funeral testified by its sorrow how keenly felt was the loss of her who, for the love of Jesus Christ, had made herself the humble servant of slaves."

She was given the title "Servant of God" by the Catholic Church in 1989 as the Church received her cause for canonization to sainthood and began the process of carefully studying her life and her prodigious works of mercy toward her poor and suffering neighbors.

Alexander Milne (1742-1838)

The most extensive epitaph to be found anywhere in New Orleans is carved into the grey granite monument marking the grave of this Scottish-born philanthropist. The epitaph shows his last will and testament as well as the wordage from a document establishing an orphanage called Milne Asylum for Destitute Boys. Milne earned his fortune in hardware and brick-making.

Epidemics sent thousands to the graveyard

Epidemics of yellow fever, plague and cholera took the lives of some 40,000 New Orleanians, primarily during the 19th century.

Many of those who died in these epidemics are remembered with markers in New Orleans' historic cemeteries. Others were buried in mass graves.

The first yellow fever epidemic occurred in 1796 with a death toll of 638. According to George Augustin's *History of Yellow Fever*, more than 5,000 people died between 1817 and 1839. The next two decades, 1840-1860, found approximately 24,000 deaths due to yellow fever. In 1853, a cholera epidemic hit New Orleans and killed 129 while yellow fever took about 8,000 lives. Between 1861 and 1905, yellow fever claimed more than 9,000 lives.

Yellow fever is transmitted by mosquitos and attacks the liver. Symptoms include jaundice, vomiting, organ failure and hemorrhaging.

Plague was brought to New Orleans by rats arriving at the Port of New Orleans on ships. Symptoms include severe fever, chills and swollen lymph nodes.

Cholera is spread through contaminated drinking water and causes diarrhea and dehydration. Many in antebellum New Orleans believed this disease was airborne, so they began burning tar to create a thick smoke, hoping to kill the infection in the air.

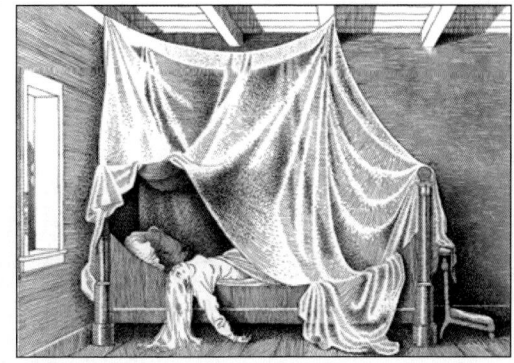

A woman dead from yellow fever lies half in and half out of her deathbed. (Historic New Orleans Collection)

Jacques Philippe Villere (1761-1830)

The second governor of Louisiana (1816-20) and the first native-born governor of the state, he served honorably as an officer in the Battle of New Orleans.

Marine Corps Major Daniel Carmick (d. 1816)

The gravesite of this distinguished military man, who fought in the Battle of New Orleans, features one of the most outstanding ornate iron enclosures in this cemetery.

Barelli Family tomb ▶

This extraordinary tomb was designed by Milan native Joseph Barelli (1801-1858) as a memorial to his son who died in a steamboat explosion in 1849 at the Mississippi River dock (about where the Riverwalk is today). The tomb depicts the explosion and the boy's soul being lifted to heaven by an angel.

CHAPTER 3

Lafayette Cemeteries 1 & 2
(Cemetery 1 – 1400 block of Washington Avenue)
(Cemetery 2 – 2110 Washington Avenue)

Lafayette Cemetery 1, located across the street from the famous Commander's Palace restaurant in the Garden District, is one of the city's most visited historic cemeteries.

Established in 1832, it was carved out of what was then the New Orleans suburb of Lafayette, a community located south of the *Vieux Carre*. Twenty years later, in 1852, Lafayette became a part of the City of New Orleans through annexation.

The cemetery land originally was part of the Livaudais plantation. Many persons of Irish and German descent are buried here, along with countless victims of the yellow fever epidemics of the mid-1800s.

Seven blocks away is the less well-known Lafayette Cemetery 2, which is in need of repairs and is located in a markedly different neighborhood.

During the yellow fever epidemics, large community burials took place at Lafayette Cemetery 1, including many German and Irish settlers. Interestingly enough, the original design for Lafayette 1 was done by Benjamin Buisson, one of Napoleon's engineers who had fled to the United States after Napoleon's army was defeated at Waterloo in 1815. Lafayette Cemetery 1 was dedicated to musician-composer Theodore von La Hache, a leading composer of Confederate songs and co-founder of the New Orleans Philharmonic Society; a plaque recognizing this dedication can be seen at the entrance.

The famous writer Anne Rice lived six blocks away from the cemetery, which served as one of the settings for some of her novels. The movie based on her book, *Interview With The Vampire*, was in part filmed here.

The Garden District stands in stark contrast to the French Quarter, which was more of a seat of Creole culture. The Garden District was mostly inhabited by the newly arrived Americans of German and Irish descent. They were Protestant and spoke English, as opposed to being French-speaking Catholics. These discrepancies caused social divisions and extreme competition in business.

The Louisiana Purchase and the economic prosperity enjoyed by the newcomers fueled the construction of New Orleans' grand upriver homes, creating a residential zone of opulence extending from the Garden District to Carrollton Avenue. The local economy was heavily dependent on agriculture, shipping and the slave trade, with New Orleans having the largest slave market in the United States.

Lafayette Cemetery 1 holds the remains of numerous persons of Irish and German descent, many of whom died of yellow fever. The tomb at left is for Jefferson Fire Company No. 22, distinguished by a relief carving of mid-1800s firefighting equipment.

Novelist Anne Rice drew inspiration from historic cemeteries

Anne Rice has spent a fair amount of time strolling through New Orleans' historic cemeteries. She's drawn inspiration from them, ideas that have helped to make her one of the most recognized novelists in the country.

Lafayette Cemetery 1 seems to be her favorite graveyard, for it is here that we find the Karstendiek Family tomb, which is the model for the tomb that plays a central role in the 1994 movie based on Rice's first and most famous novel, *Interview With The Vampire*. In the movie, this is the tomb where the vampire Lestat resides. It is where he stays when he is not out at night prowling the streets in pursuit of the blood that sustains him.

Another grave in Lafayette Cemetery 1 is said to be the model for the communal tomb of the Mayfair witches in Rice's novel, *The Witching Hour*.

This same cemetery was the setting for a staged jazz funeral in which Rice rode in a glass coffin to generate pre-publication publicity for another of her books, *Memnoch the Devil*.

Anne Rice was born in New Orleans in 1941 and was reared there. Her parents, for some reason, named her Howard Allen Frances O'Brien. Understandably, she didn't like the name, so she changed it to Anne when she entered first grade at Redemptorist Catholic School.

In addition to books involving vampires, witches, devils and mummies, Rice has written on the life of Christ, including *Christ the Lord: Out of Egypt*.

Graveyard settings such as this one were used in some of renowned author Anne Rice's novels, as well as in the movie based on her book, Interview with the Vampire.

Capt. Charles McLellan

This 22-year-old Confederate officer died defending Richmond, Virginia. The broken column bears the initials CSA, for Confederate States of America. He was from Maine, and his family is said to have shipped soil from his home state so he could be buried in Maine soil.

'The Vampire Tomb'

The grave of the fictional vampire Lestat in the movie, Interview With The Vampire, was modeled after this one, the Karstendiek Family tomb. (Photo courtesy of Save Our Cemeteries.)

Tomb of Destitute Orphans

This communal tomb is a relic of the epidemics that left large numbers of children orphaned in New Orleans in the nineteenth century. The epidemics gave rise to a profusion of orphan asylums at the time, with names such as Poydras, Milne, Fink, Sister Regis, St. Vincent's, St. Elizabeth's and the Jewish Orphan Home.

CHAPTER 4

Cypress Grove Cemetery
(120 City Park Avenue)

This cemetery was founded in 1840 by the Firemen's Charitable and Benevolent Association with money willed from a wealthy New Orleanian named Stephen Henderson. When the Girod Street Cemetery began to deteriorate, many Protestant families chose Cypress Grove, which has a deep, narrow layout with several oak-shaded areas.

Many of the tombs here are crafted in marble, granite, or cast iron and are outstanding examples of exquisite memorial architecture. Bas-relief carvings of weeping willows, angels, women in mourning and other symbols of death can be found in this cemetery. Its main entrance gate, which faces Metairie Road, was built in beautiful Egyptian Revival style. Each side of the cemetery is lined with brick wall vaults that have deteriorated over time.

◄ *A sculpture commemorates the death of the baby Albert Hall Rodd, who was seven months old when he died in 1864. His mother holds him over a baptismal font.*

Foreground: *Local foundries made rustic fences from iron starting in the 1830s in an architectural movement known as "picturesque." Here the McIntosh Family tomb is surrounded by a fence in the form of tree stumps and branches.* ►

Background: *Robert Slark, a wealthy hardware dealer, and one of his family members, W.H. Letchford, are buried in these striking monuments that resemble small churches.*

Leeds Family tomb

This rusting cast-iron tomb belongs to the family who owned the Leeds Foundry. Charles Leeds was Mayor of New Orleans in the 1870s.

Irad Ferry (1801-1837)

A broken Doric column, symbolizing a life cut short, marks the grave of Irad Ferry, a New Orleans fireman who died fighting a fire on Camp Street in 1837. This gravesite also features a carving of a vintage fire pump.

Syme-Hardy Family tomb

One of the first truly impressive sights one sees upon entering Cypress Grove Cemetery is the Syme-Hardy Family tomb, topped by an elegantly carved statue of an angelic young woman dropping a flower on the grave.

Chinese tomb of the Soon On Tong Association

This communal tomb was built in 1904, in the heyday of New Orleans' Chinatown. Originally, it was a temporary holding facility in which the remains of the deceased were kept before being sent back to China; however, this practice is no longer in use. The small fireplace against the back wall was used to burn prayer notes for the deceased.

CHAPTER 5
Dispersed of Judah Cemetery
(4937 Canal Street)

The Spanish Inquisition forbade Jews and Protestants from settling in Catholic Louisiana when it was under Spanish rule. However, some did settle here. In 1803, when the United States acquired the Louisiana territory from France, a small Jewish population was already living in New Orleans.

In 1828, the first Jewish synagogue was chartered in New Orleans, and in 1846 the city's second-oldest Jewish cemetery was begun. It is known today as Dispersed of Judah Cemetery. Many who are buried here came from the Caribbean and were from a Spanish or Portuguese Sephardic Jewish background.

The land for this cemetery was donated by Judah Touro, one of New Orleans' most active movers and shakers of the ninteenth century.

In Jewish cemeteries, all headstones face in the direction of Jerusalem, in keeping with the tradition of praying toward the Wailing Wall, which is all that remains of the Second Temple of Jerusalem, one of Judaism's holiest sites.

Some of the New Orleans Jewish community went to great lengths to memorialize their deceased loved ones. The tomb at the center of the photo on the facing page (also on this page at left) is that of Lilla Benjamin (1839-1911), who would sit in her logged chair outside the family business and encourage passersby to come in and shop.

Virginia Lazarus (d. 1897)

A life-size mournful figure stands atop the tomb of this young woman who was 18 when she died.

Moses Aletrino (1830-1895)

An elegantly carved cloaked urn tops the tomb of Moses Aletrino.

Abraham H. D'Meza

This tomb is typical of the many throughout the cemetery on which Bible verses are carved in Hebrew.

Roschen Rosenthal (1813-1905) and Family tomb

The tomb of this Jewish family who immigrated from Aurich, Germany, is distinguished by an engraved monument and two large obelisks on either side.

CHAPTER 6
Greenwood Cemetery
(5190 Canal Boulevard)

Founded in 1852 by the Firemen's Charitable and Benevolent Association, Greenwood Cemetery is one of New Orleans' largest cemeteries, being a vast 150 acres with approximately 20,000 plots and some 1,000 interments per year.

Greenwood is essentially an extension of Cypress Grove Cemetery, which is located across the street. When Cypress Grove became overcrowded because of the many deaths caused by a yellow fever epidemic, the Benevolent Association had to increase its burial space.

The Association was able to buy the land for the cemetery for firemen and their families, thanks to the generosity of Stephen Henderson, a wealthy New Orleans businessman and volunteer firefighter. He donated valuable land that the Association sold, using the proceeds to purchase property for Greenwood. Historically, New Orleans firefighters were local businessmen, including free men of color.

Near Greenwood's entrance, the tombs are mostly of brick or Georgia marble, but as one walks deeper into the cemetery, the marble gives way to granite, limestone and concrete. The lots are sold today to include perpetual care – something that wasn't offered in the cemetery's early years.

J.M. Pelton Family tomb

A 19th century cast iron tomb entrance depicts an angel with a comforting arm around a woman. This piece was created by the Robert Wood firm of Philadelphia and the Miltenberger Foundry of New Orleans.

Benevolent & Protective Order of Elks Lodge No. 30 tumulus

Located at the main entrance of the cemetery is a bronze statue of an elk atop a grassy mound. Under the elk – which is the symbol of the fraternity – is a Doric-style marble chamber with 18 burial vaults sealed with bronze doors.

Firemen's Charitable Association monument

Erected in 1887, this 46-foot-tall granite structure is enclosed within Gothic arches. It was designed by stonemason Charles Orleans and probably modeled after the Sir Walter Scott memorial in Edinburgh, Scotland. The statue in the center depicts a fireman with his hose, gazing out over the historically fire-ravaged city

Confederate monument

Erected in 1874 through the efforts of the Ladies Benevolent Association of Louisiana, this monument marks the mass grave of 600 Confederate soldiers. On each side of the base is a marble likeness of a Confederate general: "Stonewall" Jackson, Robert E. Lee, Leonidas Polk and Albert S. Johnston. At the top is a 7-foot marble statue of a Confederate soldier, carved in Italy.

Santa Rosalia Society tomb

This society was started in 1902 to honor St. Rosalia, who is credited with helping Sicily survive the Black Plague epidemic of 1620. In 1899, during an anthrax outbreak among cattle in a rural area outside of New Orleans, Sicilian immigrants prayed for help through the intercession of St. Rosalia.

CHAPTER 7
St. Louis Cemetery 3
(3421 Esplanade Ave.)

Established in 1854, the year after a devastating yellow fever epidemic, St. Louis 3 is the largest of the three St. Louis cemeteries. This site was once known as "Lepers Land," because in the eighteenth century Louisiana Governor Galvez exiled lepers to this location, where later they died and were buried.

The entrance is marked by a set of heavy iron gates, typical of New Orleans ironwork. The cemetery is heavily populated, with about 400 interments a year.

The main aisles are named after saints, the center being named after St. Louis and the other two aisles for St. Peter and St. Paul. The cross-aisles are named for bishops and archbishops. During the late nineteenth and early twentieth centuries, it was fashionable to decorate the tops of tombs with sculpted

Bellocq Family tomb

E.J. Bellocq was known for his haunting photographs of the prostitutes of Storyville, which inspired several novels, poems and films. Only after his death were his pictures revealed to the public.

Italian marble angels; most are stock figures, but some were custom-made. This is why you will see so many angels in the cemetery.

Notable citizens buried here include Thomy Lafon (1810–1893), a highly educated, tri-lingual humanitarian and free person of color who made a fortune in real estate. Also interred are Ernest "Dutch" Morial, the first African-American mayor of New Orleans, and numerous nuns and sisters from several Catholic religious congregations. There is also a "Chef's Corner," where restaurateur families such as Tujague, Prudhomme and Galatoire have been laid to rest.

Fourchy Family tomb

This tomb features a heartrending statue of a grieving mother holding her deceased child on her lap.

Hellenic Orthodox community tomb

Situated in the Greek Orthodox section of the cemetery is the elegant Hellenic Orthodox community tomb.

Ernest "Dutch" Morial (1929-1989)

He was the first black mayor of New Orleans and the first African-American person to graduate from the LSU Law School. During his tenure, the Riverfront Streetcar line was established and the Warehouse District was revitalized into the cultural/artistic hub it is today. In 1992, the Ernest N. Morial Convention Center was named in his honor. In 2014, 25 years after his death, his family had his remains moved from St. Louis Cemetery 1 to this more spacious site in St. Louis 3.

Sisters of St. Joseph tomb

This tomb is topped by a statue of St. Joseph, the husband of Mary, the mother of Jesus.

Servants of Mary tomb

A statue of the Blessed Virgin Mary, mother of Jesus, helps to identify the graves of members of the Catholic religious order known as the Servants of Mary.

Dante Masonic Lodge tomb

A Free Mason lodge, established in New Orleans in 1865, was named for the famous Italian poet Dante Alighieri, who is considered the father of the Italian language. Members of the lodge are entombed here.

James Gallier Sr. (1795-1866)

One of New Orleans' most talented architects, James Gallier, and his wife died in a storm at sea while on a voyage from New York to New Orleans. Gallier Hall in downtown New Orleans was designed by him and is used today for Mardi Gras balls and other social events.

CHAPTER 8
Hebrew Rest Cemetery
(2003 Pelopidas Street at Frenchman Street)

Hebrew Rest was founded in 1860 by the congregation Shangarai Chasset. It is the largest Jewish cemetery in New Orleans and has some of the most impressive tombs and obelisks.

The grounds are well manicured and the entrance features skillfully crafted iron gates. Today, it is owned by the Temple Sinai congregation and Touro Synagogue, which is the successor of Shangarai Chasset.

This cemetery holds the remains of many pioneer Jews of German background. Their burial traditions are rooted in ancient Hebrew customs of in-ground burial. The high water table and abundance of annual rainfall in New Orleans posed a problem for in-ground burial. However, by using one- to two-foot-high frames – called copings – filled with soil Jews were able to bury their deceased in raised beds so that the bodies are in fact buried in the earth.

It was not until after the Louisiana Purchase of 1803, when New Orleans became a busy international seaport, that there was substantial Jewish immigration to the city. Before then, the Inquisition forbade Jews and Protestants from settling in Catholic Louisiana. Some of nineteenth century New Orleans' most active movers and shakers were of Jewish descent.

The ancient Jewish tradition of in-ground burial is observed in Hebrew Rest Cemetery. The well-organized property features special touches such as a circular garden topped with a statue of a child.

A life-size winged angel stands atop a grave of two
Levi family members, who died at the young ages of 18 and 21.

Harriette Levi (1844-1883)

A large white bronze monument bears a fair likeness of Mrs. Levi, a New Orleans native.

Gumbel Family tomb

Replicas of three sacks–possibly modeled after those found in cottonseed oil mills–are engraved with the names of Gumbel children. These are three of the 11 children of Simon and Sophie Gumbel, who were wealthy Jews and natives of Bavaria. Simon Gumbel made a fortune in the cottonseed oil business and in real estate.

The largest Jewish cemetery in New Orleans, Hebrew Rest includes numerous impressive tombs and obelisks.

Marx Family plot

Like many of the burial spaces in Hebrew Rest Cemetery, the Marx Family plot features a simple design and is well maintained.

Chapter 9
Masonic Cemetery
(400 City Park Avenue)

The Masonic Cemetery was founded in 1865, soon after the Civil War, by the Grand Lodge of Louisiana, which was comprised of Free and Accepted Masons. At the time, the city was under military occupation.

Records indicate the existence of Masonic Lodges in New Orleans as early as the 1730s. Well-known Masons in Louisiana included William Claiborne, Louisiana's first governor, and Oscar J. Dunn, the state's first black lieutenant governor. Historically, the Masons of New Orleans have been more racially integrated than other such groups around the country.

The stated principles of Freemasonry include political compromise and religious tolerance, which is why totalitarian governments have often tried to prohibit them. Many famous Europeans were Freemasons, including French philosopher Voltaire, German writer and statesman Johann von Goethe, and musical composer Joseph Haydn. In the U.S., George Washington and several of the signers of the Declaration of Independence were Freemasons.

Fraternal societies have existed throughout much of civilization, and burial of their members is one of their responsibilities. One of the most well-known fraternal organizations in the United States today is the Freemasons, which was established by the Grand Lodge of Masons in London in 1717. However, some recognize the Masonic fraternity as having medieval origins, and others trace it back even further.

Most Masonic Lodges bury their dead in copings, which are frames made of stone or brick and plaster and filled with soil. Masons are thus buried in the earth.

Pinckard tomb

This distinctive gravesite incorporates several elegant architectural elements, including a chapel theme and checkerboard-patterned tile on the main approach to the tomb.

The Perfect Union Lodge 1 tomb

This old tomb was built in a highly unusual Gothic design with a large stairway going up to its roof. The other three sides of the tomb feature a chapel-like motif. Inside are vaults on either side of a corridor.

Brennan and Holdsworth Family tomb

Two prominent Masonic families are commemorated with this elegantly carved tomb.

Red River Pilots Assn. tomb

With a steamboat wheel adorning its pediment, this tomb holds the remains of members of an alliance of steamboat pilots who plied the rivers between New Orleans and Shreveport during the 19th century.

Several members of Osiris Masonic Lodge No. 300 have been buried in this plot, which can be found easily because of its tall, distinctive markers.

CHAPTER 10

Metairie/Lake Lawn Cemetery
(5100 Pontchartrain Boulevard)

This unique 150-acre cemetery, which sits on the site of the former Metairie Race Course, is home to the largest collection of marble tombs and statues in the New Orleans metropolitan area. Named Metairie Cemetery in 1872, it is the final resting place for numerous Civil War soldiers.

Its designer, Colonel Benjamin Morgan Henry, worked with the racetrack design, retaining meticulous landscaping and wide-open spaces. His vision was to make it more park-like and spacious than other New Orleans area cemeteries, which were crowded and surrounded by wall vaults. Another feature which enhanced its beauty was the addition of two lakes — Horseshoe Lake, which was part of Bayou Metairie, and Lake Prospects, which exists today as a lagoon.

In 1969, an addition was made to the original grounds by annexing the adjacent Lake Lawn Park.

Here one can find the gravesites of political leaders and many of New Orleans' most influential families. For instance, Confederate President Jefferson Davis; Confederate general P. G. T. Beauregard; former New Orleans Mayor deLesseps "Chep" Morrison; Tom Benson, the long-time owner of the New Orleans Saints NFL team; the founders of Jackson Brewing Company and Popeye's Fried Chicken and the co-founder of K & B Drugstores; plus nine governors, including Louisiana's first African-American governor, Pickney Benton Stewart Pinchback, who founded Southern University for the education of minority students.

Chas F. Beck tomb

Mourning angels and bereaved descendants are depicted elegantly on numerous graves throughout the cemetery.

Babette Vonderbank Ahrens (1852-1928)

This is a stunning polished red granite monument with a cloaked bronze statue and a portrait plaque of Mrs. Vonderbank, a German immigrant. Looking on are grieving life-size bronze look-alikes of her niece and nephew. The nephew is holding his hat in one hand out of respect and holding his sister's hand with the other.

Al Copeland grave (1944-2008)

The founder of Popeye's Fried Chicken, Al Copeland was born into poverty before building his business empire of more than 700 restaurants worldwide, beginning in New Orleans in 1972.

Fabacher Family tomb

This family owned and operated the Jackson Brewing Company, makers of the famous JAX beer, a New Orleans favorite.

Moriarty monument

The gravesite of the Moriarty Family is marked by the most imposing monument in the cemetery; it is 60 feet tall. The statues represent Faith, Hope, Charity and Memory.

Delgado Family tomb

This commanding canopied granite tomb was built in 1905 by Albert Weiblen. The Delgados were sugar planters of Sephardic Jewish origin who left a fortune to help found Delgado Community College, the original Charity Hospital, and the Delgado Museum (now known as the New Orleans Museum of Art).

Rogers, Palfrey and Brewster Family

This 15-foot-high stonework Celtic cross was inspired by designs of crosses erected in Ireland. It features exquisite details of various Christian symbols, including the Holy Spirit (in the form of a dove), the True Vine, and the Eucharistic cup of Jesus.

Besthoff Family tomb

The elegant tomb of the Besthoff Family features four columns topped with a replica of King Solomon's crown and guarded by two large angels. The once famous K&B drugstores (Katz & Besthoff) of New Orleans were co-founded by this family. The stores were sold to the Rite Aid chain in 1972.

◀ John Henry Maginnis Family tomb

This is a stately tomb with beautiful iron doors and a life-size wingless angel on top holding a cross. The family owned a successful cotton mill in New Orleans' Warehouse District. John Henry Maginnis died in 1889 and was interred here.

Aldigé Family tomb

Three family members entombed here were lost in the tragic sinking of the steamship SS La Bourgogne in 1898. A distraught winged angel stands guard on top of the tomb; the base of the sculpture is in the shape of a boat and anchor.

Harrington tomb **Ada Mattingly (1864-1936)**

Statues of angels and women in mourning are plentiful in this thought-provoking cemetery.
At left is the final resting place of a famous poker-faced gambler nick-named "Never Smile" Harrington.
At right the grave of Ada Mattingly is topped by a mournful angel kneeling under a large cross.

82 Cities of the Dead

Capt. Jose Morales / Josie Arlington

This tomb was built originally for Josie Arlington (1864-1914), the most famous madam of the Storyville red-light district of New Orleans. The family of Capt. Jose Morales (1925-2006) later bought the tomb, and Josie's remains were moved to an unmarked grave.

Metairie/Lake Lawn **83**

Edith Allen Clark (1883-1965)

Built in the 1960s, this monument is a large polished black granite block to which is attached a bronze Pieta showing the Virgin Mary holding the lifeless body of her son, Jesus. The art was done by sculptor Felix de Weldon, creator of the Iwo Jima monument in Washington, D.C.

Chapman H. Hyams (1838-1923)

He was a millionaire stock broker, art collector and philanthropist who had this Greek temple mausoleum built for his sisters. Inside, sunlight streaming through two blue stained glass windows casts a beautiful blue light on the marble statue of a grief-stricken angel leaning over an altar.

James Blitch Sr. (1923-1998)

A beautiful wire version of the Holy Family graces this tomb. James Blitch was an architect whose work includes Grace King High School, Chateau de Notre Dame, Children's Hospital and East Jefferson Hospital. His ancestors built Oak Alley plantation, on the Mississippi River west of New Orleans.

Lucien Brunswig (d. 1892)

Designed after an Egyptian Revival-style tomb in Munich, Germany, this tomb holds the remains of a German wholesale drug merchant. Standing before the grilled bronze entrance is a life-size marble woman extending her hand toward the family name. A marble sphinx also serves as an eternal guardian.

Army of Northern Virginia monument

This 50-foot granite monument was erected in 1881 in memory of the men of the Army of Northern Virginia who fought in the Civil War. A statue of Gen. "Stonewall" Jackson stands on top. The remains of the President of the Confederacy, Jefferson Davis, were interred here when he died in 1889; his funeral was the largest in New Orleans history.

Washington Artillery, Louisiana Branch monument

This monument commemorates the Louisiana men who died in the Civil War while serving in the Washington Artillery. On top is a likeness of James B. Walton, the commander of the unit. On the sides are the unit's logo, a laurel-wreathed tiger's head, a bust of George Washington, and the Louisiana state seal.

Capt. Salvatore Pizzati (1839-1915)

He was a wealthy merchant who made a fortune importing tropical fruit. This ornate mausoleum is embellished with medieval turrets, Byzantine columns, curved dentils, a large statue of Memory, elegantly carved garlands, and an alpha and omega symbol in front.

Tom Benson (1927-2018)

This is the tomb of the longtime owner of the NFL's New Orleans Saints and the NBA's New Orleans Pelicans. A noted philanthropist, especially in support of Catholic institutions and organizations, Tom Benson graduated from Jesuit-run Loyola University in 1948, after serving in the U.S. Navy in 1945. (After many years of mostly losing seasons, Benson's beloved pro football team won the Super Bowl in 2010; it was one of the greatest joys of his life. And for many long-suffering Saints fans, the victory was like dying and going to heaven!)

CHAPTER 11
St. Roch Cemetery
(1725 St. Roch Avenue)

Saint Roch Cemetery was established in 1874 by a German-born priest named Fr. Peter Thevis, who arrived in New Orleans amid a yellow fever epidemic. He became pastor of Holy Trinity Catholic Church in lower New Orleans.

Fr. Thevis and his congregation prayed for St. Roch's intercession, for healing and protection from yellow fever. They all were spared from the disease. He made good on his promise to build a chapel and cemetery named for St. Roch along with a shrine to the saint. When Fr. Thevis died, his remains were buried under the floor of the chapel in front of the altar.

St. Roch was born around 1295 in France and was a devoutly religious man. It was reported that he performed miraculous cures during epidemics of the Black Death in Europe. It is believed by some that Rome was spared from the plague due to his prayers.

St. Roch's Chapel was built in Gothic Revival style. The approach to the chapel is highlighted by a lifelike image of the crucified Christ and a beautiful marble carving of a sick girl whose life ultimately was spared. Over the years, hundreds of pilgrims have come to this site and left votive offerings of crutches, braces and models of limbs in gratitude for healings they credited to St. Roch's intercession. These items are on display in a room at the side of the shrine. (These objects are known as *ex-votos*, which are offerings to

Saint Roch

the saint in gratitude for favors received.) One will also see the words "Thanks" or "*Merci*" inscribed into the marble tiles that pave the floor in this room.

The cemetery is walled with burial vaults and has several enclaves with Italian marble statues depicting the Stations of the Cross.

In 1879, another section was added to the cemetery on its eastern side. It is known as St. Roch Cemetery 2 and includes a beautiful chapel called St. Michael's that is also used as a mausoleum.

The main entrance to St. Roch Cemetery features iron gates framed by stone columns topped by angel sentinels keeping watch.

The approach to the Chapel of St. Roch is graced with a large crucifix overlooking a marble statue of a sick girl who symbolizes the many who were affected by the yellow fever epidemics of the 1800s.

This well-maintained alley of above-ground graves is found in St. Roch Cemetery, which is named for the patron saint for protection against the plague.

On the side of the Shrine of St. Roch is a room full of votive offerings to the 14th century saint, including crutches and braces, in appreciation for the healings believed to be achieved through his intercession. The floor is paved with marble tiles inscribed with expressions of gratitude to God and to St. Roch.

St. Roch, protector against the plague

St. Roch (1295-1327) was born in Montpellier, France, to elderly parents. Something of a miracle baby, at birth he was marked with a deep red cross on his side, foreshadowing his Christ-centered life.

He spent his youth in prayer, penance and charity, giving to the poor all of his considerable inheritance. He joined the Third Order of St. Francis (known today as the Secular Franciscan Order) and began working with the plague-stricken without fear of contagion, believing that "with God, nothing is impossible." He blessed the sick – thousands of them – with the Sign of the Cross, and they were cured. He is said even to have cured animals who came to him seeking relief from the disease.

On his deathbed, his final words were a prayer:

"I humbly beseech thee, Lord, that whosoever is attacked by the plague, or is in danger of being attacked, and shall implore my protection with faith, may be delivered from this sickness.... I solicit this grace...in the name of thy mercy and clemency, which are infinite."

St. Roch is the patron saint against the plague; he is also known as the patron of dogs, dog lovers and falsely accused persons.

Source: Saint Conrad and Saint Roch, Third Order of St. Francis, by Fr. Hilarion Duerk, OFM, booklet published in 1919.

An image of the crucified Christ is featured outside St. Michael's Chapel Mausoleum in St. Roch Cemetery 2.

Marble statues imported from Italy depict the Stations of the Cross, which are positioned in protective enclaves in the cemetery.

~In Memoriam~
The New Orleans Katrina Memorial

A section of Charity Hospital Cemetery, located at 5050 Canal St., was set aside to commemorate the lives of 83 unidentified and unclaimed people who died in Hurricane Katrina in 2005, primarily from drowning. The hurricane, described as "the worst natural disaster in U.S. history," caused levees to break and seawalls to collapse, which resulted in the flooding of 80 percent of the city. In all, Katrina killed some 1,800 people in southeast Louisiana and on the Mississippi Gulf Coast.

THE NEW ORLEANS KATRINA MEMORIAL

ON AUGUST 29, 2005, HURRICANE KATRINA MADE LANDFALL UPON THE LOUISIANA AND MISSISSIPPI GULF COAST, BRINGING DEVASTATION TO MANY COMMUNITIES. IN NEW ORLEANS, STORM SURGE AND THE FAILURE OF THE LEVEE SYSTEM CAUSED FLOODING IN OVER EIGHTY PERCENT OF THE CITY, TRAPPING THOUSANDS. IN THE CHAOTIC AFTERMATH, NEW ORLEANIANS FACED DESPERATE CIRCUMSTANCES IN HOMES, HOSPITALS, THE SUPERDOME AND OTHER MAKESHIFT SHELTERS. DESPITE THE HEROIC EFFORTS OF FIRST RESPONDERS, MEDICAL PERSONNEL, VOLUNTEERS AND THE MILITARY, OVER 1,100 CITIZENS LOST THEIR LIVES IN THE DISASTER.

MOST OF THE DECEASED WERE IDENTIFIED AND BURIED BY LOVED ONES IN PRIVATE CEREMONIES THROUGHOUT THE NATION. HERE LIE THE REMAINING, THE UNCLAIMED AND UNIDENTIFIED VICTIMS OF THE STORM FROM THE NEW ORLEANS AREA. SOME HAVE BEEN FORGOTTEN. SOME REMAIN UNKNOWN.

THIS MEMORIAL IS DEDICATED TO THESE INDIVIDUALS AND TO ALL WHO SUFFERED OR DIED DURING HURRICANE KATRINA. LET THE VICTIMS HERE FOREVER REMIND US OF THOSE HARROWING DAYS AND THE LONG STRUGGLE TO REBUILD OUR CITY. LET THEIR FINAL RESTING PLACE CALL US TO CONSTANT PREPAREDNESS. LET THEIR SOULS JOIN INTO AN ETERNAL CHORUS, SINGING WITH THE FULL MIGHT OF THE INDOMITABLE SPIRIT OF NEW ORLEANS.

JEFFREY ROUSE, M.D., CHIEF DEPUTY CORONER
AUGUST 29, 2009

Cemeteries of Greater New Orleans

These are among the most intriguing and historically rich cemeteries in the Greater New Orleans Area.

1. St. Louis 1
2. St. Louis 2
3. Lafayette 1 & 2
4. Cypress Grove
5. Greenwood
6. Dispersed of Judah
7. St. Louis 3
8. Hebrew Rest
9. Masonic
10. Metairie/Lake Lawn
11. St. Roch

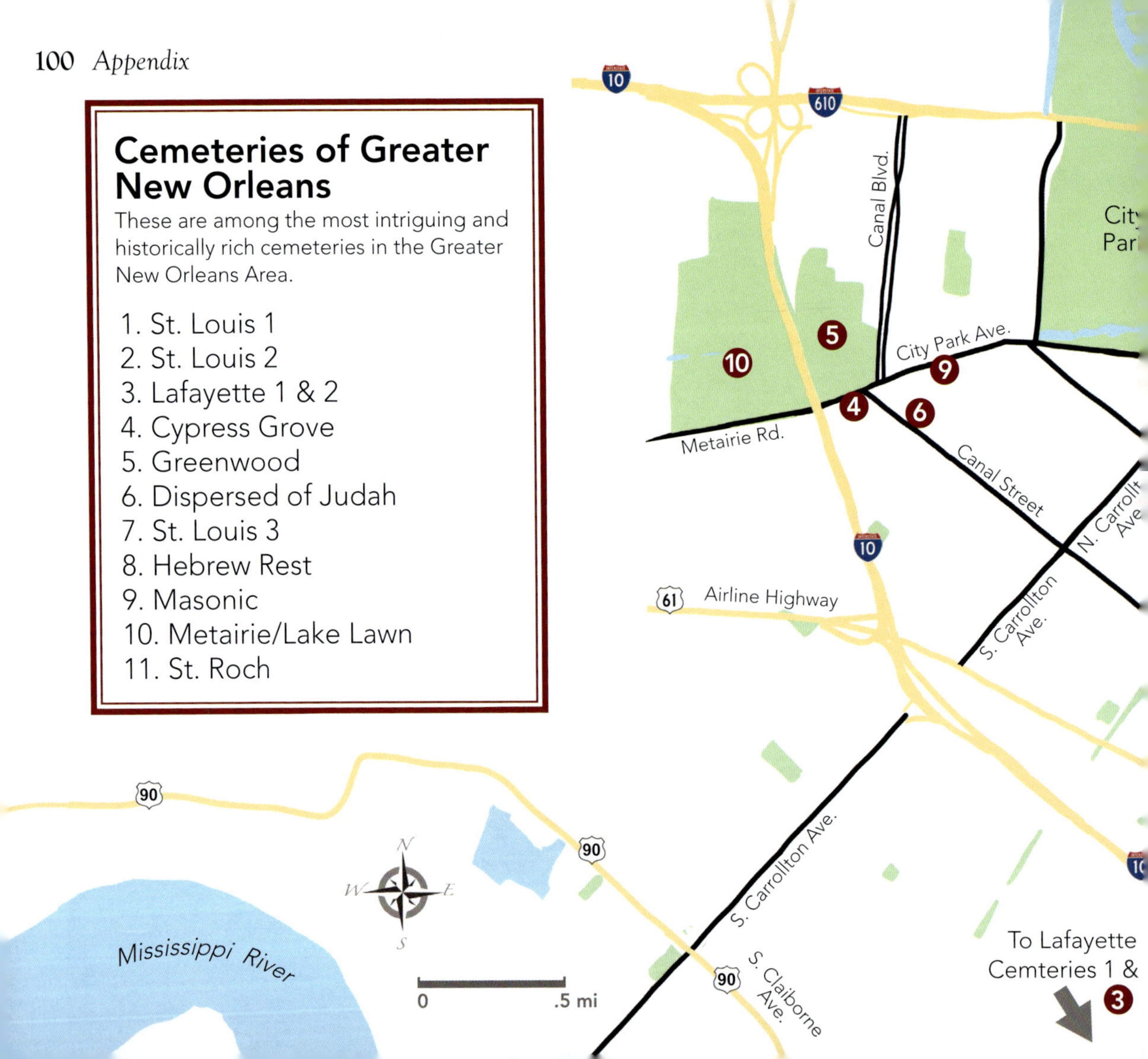

To Lafayette Cemteries 1 & 3

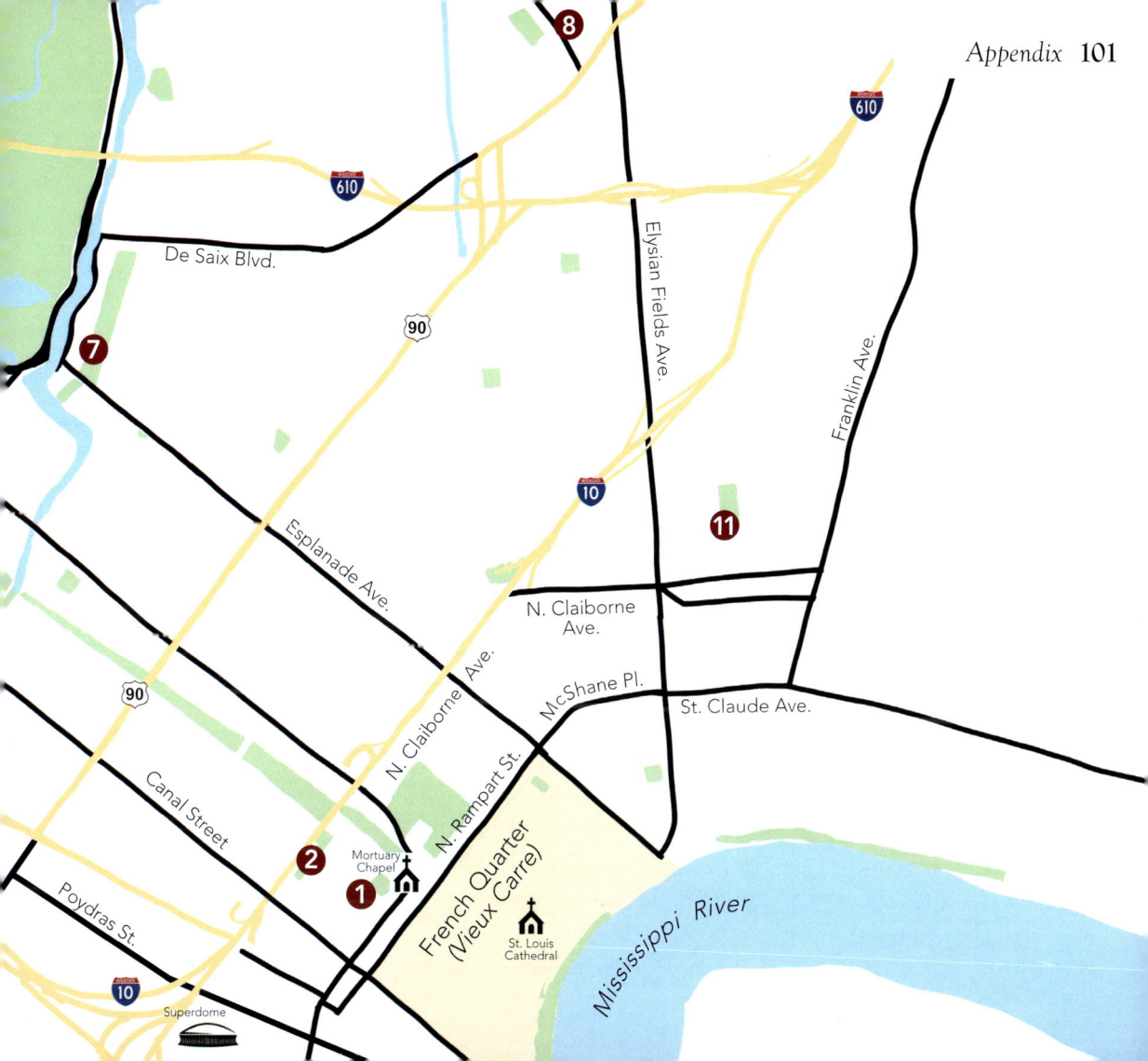

Appendix 2

Types of burial tombs

Wall vaults – These serve as the outer walls of some cemeteries in New Orleans. They are also called "oven vaults," because they resemble old-fashioned ovens. Many of the vaults have sunken and lean slightly, much like many of the buildings in New Orleans. In the past, wall vaults usually were not owned, but rented; today they are owned.

Family/private tombs – A family purchases a plot of land and builds a tomb, or they buy a tomb that has already been constructed. Most have two vaults, which are used over and over. The Creole custom of using a single vault for a number of entombments is one that always catches the curiosity of visitors. What occurs is that the remains of the latest occupant of the vault are gathered and pushed to the back; and the decayed casket wood is removed and burned, leaving space for another casket.

Private tombs usually consist of two vaults, one above the other, and a pit (*caveau*), or receptacle, below. In the past, a family could rent a wall vault as a temporary site if the private tomb was full and more than one member died within a year and a day. Many family tombs look similar to old townhouses or "shotgun" homes occupied by many New Orleanians today.

Step tombs – This is a low-lying grave with "stepped" sides, resembling steps, going up to a flat top. Bricks are laid in a pyramid shape, and the casket is placed in the opening. These tombs are used only once; they lack stability and sink in relatively short order.

Copings – These are 1- to 2-foot-high frames made of stone or brick and plaster that are filled with soil to enable the family to bury their dead in the earth, as opposed to above ground. In-ground burial is an ancient religious tradition that is observed in New Orleans by Jewish people and Freemasons.

Appendix 3

Timeline

Significant dates in the history of New Orleans

1718	**Founding of New Orleans** – Founded by the French, later handed over to Spain, returned to the French, then sold to the U.S. The founder was Jean-Baptiste Le Moyne, Sieur de Bienville, governor of French Louisiana.
1755-83	**American Revolution** – The war for American independence from Great Britain, rejecting British rule over the 13 original colonies.
1788	**First great New Orleans fire** – It destroyed the original Cabildo and most major buildings of the French Quarter, e.g., 856 of the city's 1,100 buildings.
1798	**Second great New Orleans fire** – It destroyed or damaged 212 buildings, including the jail.
1803	**Louisiana Purchase** – France sold to the U.S. 828,000 square miles of land, nearly doubling the size of the U.S. This land was later divided into 15 states. Price: $11.25 million and another $3.75 million in credits.
1812	**Louisiana statehood declared** on April 30, 1812.
1812	**War of 1812** – Considered "the second war for independence" from Great Britain; declaration of war signed on June 18, 1812.
1815	**Battle of New Orleans** – Andrew Jackson leads a bloody assault on the British army–not knowing that the Treaty of Ghent had been signed two weeks earlier
1819	**Yellow fever** epidemic kills over 2,000 people in New Orleans.
1853	**Yellow fever** kills nearly 8,000 people while cholera claims 129 lives.
1858	**Yellow fever** kills over 4,800 in New Orleans.
1861-65	**Civil War** – Some 620,000 soldiers are killed in battle in the War Between the States. Officially, war began on April 12, 1861, with the firing on Fort Sumter and ended April 9, 1865, with Gen. Grant accepting Gen. Lee's surrender at the Appomattox, Virginia, Court House. Five days later, President Lincoln was assassinated.

Sources

Books and other printed documents

Arrigo, Jan and McElroy, Laura. *Cemeteries of New Orleans: A Journey through the Cities of the Dead.* Vancouver, B.C.: Voyageur Press, 2005.

Brock, Eric. *Images of America: New Orleans Cemeteries.* Charleston, S.C.: Arcadia Publishing, 1999.

Duerk, Hilarion, OFM. *Saint Conrad and Saint Roch, Third Order of St. Francis.* 1919.

Huber, Leonard, McDowell, P., and Christovich, M. L. *New Orleans Architecture: Vol. III, The Cemeteries.* Gretna, La.: Pelican Publishing, 2004.

Florence, Robert. *City of the Dead: A Journey through St. Louis Cemetery #1, New Orleans, Louisiana.* Lafayette, La.: The Center for Louisiana Studies, 1996.

Florence, Robert and Florence, Mason. *New Orleans Cemeteries: Life in the Cities of the Dead.* New Orleans: Batture Press, 2005.

Online

Black, Annetta. "Metairie Cemetery." *Atlas Obscura*, October 18, 2013. http://www.atlasobscura.com/places/metairie-cemetery-new-orleans.

"Judah Touro (1775-1854)." *Jewish Virtual Library: A Project of AICE*, American-Israeli Cooperative Enterprise, https://www.jewishvirtuallibrary.org/judah-touro.

Kelley, Laura. "Yellow Fever in Louisiana." *64 Parishes*, Encyclopedia of Louisiana, January 16, 2011. http://www.64parishes.org/entry/yellow-fever-in-louisiana.

Kingsley, Karen. "Cypress Grove Cemetery." *64 Parishes*, Encyclopedia of Louisiana, November 28, 2014. http://www.64parishes.org/entry/cypress-grove-cemetery.

Laurence, Alison and Lee, John. "Wharf Rats, the Plague, and Public Health," *New Orleans Historical*, https://neworleanshistorical.org/items/show/131.

"Plague." *Plague Annual Report*, Louisiana Office of Public Health - Infectious Disease Epidemiology Section, 2018, http://www.ldh.la.gov/assets/oph/Center-PHCH/Center-CH/infectious-epi/Annuals/Plague_LaIDAnnual.pdf.

"Saint Roch." *Roman Catholic Saints*, 2011, http://www.roman-catholic-saints.com/saint-roch.html.

"Yellow Fever Deaths in New Orleans, 1817-1905." *Louisiana Division, New Orleans Public Library*, http://www.nutrias.org/facts/feverdeaths.htm.

Index

NOTE: Page numbers in bold italic refer to photographs and/or their captions

African-Americans, *13*, 21, *24*, 55, *57*, 72
    free people of color, ix, *12–13*, *24–25*, 48, 55
    slavery, ix, *13*, *24–25*, 31
Ahrens, Babette Vonderbank, *74*
Aldigé Family tomb, *80*
Aletrino, Moses, *45*
Alley of graves, *93*
Arlington, Josie, *82*
Army of Northern Virginia monument, *86*
Augustin, George, 27

Barelli Family tomb, *29*
Beauregard, Confederate General P.G.T., 72
Bellocq, E.J., *54*
Bellocq Family tomb, *54*
Benevolent & Protective Order of Elks Lodge No. 30 tomb, *50*
Benjamin, Lilla, *42–43*
Benson, Tom, ix, *89*
Besthoff Family tomb, ix, *79*

Blitch, James, Sr., 85
Brennan and Holdsworth Family tomb, *69*
Brewster Family plot. *See* Rogers, Palfrey and Brewster Family plot
Brown vs. Board of Education, *14*
Brunswig, Lucien, *85*
Buisson, Benjamin, 30

Cage, Nicolas, viii, *15*
Carmick, Marine Corps Major Daniel, *29*
Cemeteries
    history reflected in, viii, ix
    map, 100–101
    (*See also* particular cemeteries in this index; tombs)
Chapel of St. Michael, 91, *96*
Chapel of St. Roch, 90, *92*
Charity Hospital Cemetery, 98
Chas F. Beck tomb, *73*
Chef's Corner, 55
Chinese Soon On Tong Association tomb, ix, *40-41*
Cholera, 27, 103

Claiborne, William, 66
Clark, Edith Allen, *83*
Communal tombs, ix, 32, *35, 40-41*
Confederate monuments, viii, *34*, 52, *52, 86*-87
Confederate soldiers, viii
Copeland, Al, ix, *75*
Copings, 60, 66, 102
Cypress Grove Cemetery, 36–41, 100

Dante Masonic Lodge, ix, *59*
Davis, Confederate President Jefferson, 72, *86*
de Boré, Jean Etienne, 13
Delgado Family tomb, ix, 77
Delille, Mother Henriette, "Servant of God," *25*
Dieu Nous Protégé Society (God Protect Us Society) tomb, ix, *13*
Dispersed of Judah Cemetery, 42–47, 100
D'Meza, Abraham H., *46*
Dunn, Oscar J., 66

Epidemics, 27

Fabacher Family tomb, ix, *75*
Family tombs, 102
  (See also particular tombs and plots in this index)
Ferguson, Judge John H., viii
Ferry, Irad, *38*
Firefighters, viii
Firemen's Charitable and Benevolent Association, 36, 48
Firemen's Charitable Association monument, *51*
Firemen's Charitable Association tomb, ix
Fourchy Family tomb, *55*
Free Masons, *59*, 66, 102

Gaines, Myra Clark, *15*
Galatoire Family, 55
Gallier, James, Sr., *59*
Galvez, Governor, 54
German burials, 30–31, *31*, *47*, 60, 66, *74*, *85*, 90
Goethe, Johann von, 66
Greek Orthodox section, St. Louis Cemetery 3, *56*
Greenwood Cemetery, 48–53, 100
Gumbel Family tomb, *63*

Hardy Family tomb. *See* Syme-Hardy Family tomb
Harrington tomb ("Never Smile" Harrington), *81*
Hebrew Rest Cemetery, ix, 60–65, 101
Hellenic Orthodox Community tomb, *56*
Henderson, Stephen, 36, 48
Henry, Colonel Benjamin Morgan, 72
History of Yellow Fever (Augustin), 27
Holdsworth Family tomb. *See* Brennan and Holdsworth Family tomb
Hyams, Chapman H., *84*

In-ground burials, 60, *61*, 66, 102
In Memoriam, 98
Interview With The Vampire (Rice), viii, 30, 32, *33*
Irish burials, 30–31, *31*
Italian Mutual Benefit Society tomb, ix, *19*

JAX Beer, ix, *75*
Jefferson Fire Company No. 22 tomb, *32*
Jewish cemeteries, 42–47, 60–65

Karstendiek Family tomb, viii, *34*
Katrina Hurricane Memorial, *98-99*

La Hache, Theodore von, 30
Lafayette Cemeteries 1 & 2, 30–35, 100
Lafon, Thomy, 55
Lanusse-McCarthy Family tomb, *21*
Laveau, Marie ("Voodoo Queen"), viii, 13
Lazarus, Virginia, *44*
Leeds, Charles, *38*
Leeds Family tomb, *38*
Lepers Land, 54
LeRiche, Antoine Phillip, 20–21
Lestat (vampire), viii, *34*
Letchford, W.H., *36–37*
Levi, Harriette, *63*
Levi Family tomb, ix, *62*

Maginnis Family tomb (John Henry Maginnis Family), *79*
Map, 101–102
Marie Laveau ("Voodoo Queen"), *12*
Martin, Francois Xavier, 20
Marx Family plot, *65*
Masonic Cemetery, 66–71, 100
Masons. *See* Free Masons
Mattingly, Ada, *81*
McIntosh Family tomb, *36–37*
McLellan, Capt. Charles, *34*
Metairie/Lake Lawn Cemetery, 72–89, 100
Milne, Alexander, 26

Index

Morales, Capt. Jose, *82*
Morial, Ernest "Dutch," viii, 55, *57*
Moriarty Family monument, *76*
Mayor deLesseps "Chep" Morrison, 72
Mortuary Chapel of Saint Anthony (Our Lady of Guadalupe church), *19*

New Orleans timeline, 103
New Orleans Hurricane Katrina Memorial, *98-99*
New Orleans Saints, ix, 72, *89*

Orleans, Charles, *51*
Osiris Masonic Lodge No. 300 plot, *71*
Our Lady of Guadalupe church (Mortuary Chapel of Saint Anthony), *19*

Palfrey Family plot. *See* Rogers, Palfrey and Brewster Family plot
Pelton Family tomb (J.M. Pelton family), ix, *49*
Pinchback, Pickney Benton Stewart, 72
Pinckard tomb, *67*
Pizzati, Capt. Salvatore, ix, *88*
Plague, 27
Plessy, Homer, viii, 13, *14*

Plessy *vs.* Ferguson, viii, *14*
Popeye's, ix, 72, *75*
Pouilly, J. N. B. de, 12, 20
Protestant cemeteries, *17*, 31, 36-41
Prudhomme Family, 55

Red River Pilots Association tomb, *70*
Rice, Anne, viii, 30, 32, *32-33*
Robinson, Carl D., M.D., (photographer), 109
Robinson, Jenny N., APRN (author), 109
Rodd, Albert Hall, *36*
Rogers, Palfrey and Brewster Family plot, *78*
Rosenthal Family tomb, *47*

Santa Rosalia Society tomb, *53*
Secular Franciscan Order, 95
Sephardic burials, 42, *77*
Servants of Mary, ix, *58*
Shangarai Chasset Congregation, 60
Shrine of St. Roch, *94*
Sisters of St. Joseph, ix, *58*
Sisters of the Holy Family, ix, *24*
Slark, Robert, *36-37*
Society for the Relief of Destitute Orphan Boys tomb, ix, *35*
Soon On Tong Association tomb, ix, *40-41*

St. Francis, 95
St. Louis Cathedral, *18, 19*
St. Louis Cemetery 1, 12-18, 101
St. Louis Cemetery 2, 20-25, 28-29, 101
St. Louis Cemetery 3, 54-59, 101
St. Michael, Chapel of, 90, *96*
St. Peter Street Cemetery, 12
St. Roch, 90, *90*, 91, *92, 94-95*
St. Roch, Chapel of, 90, *92*
St. Roch, Shrine of, *94*
St. Roch Cemetery, 90-99, *91, 93, 96,* 101
St. Roch Cemetery 2, 91, *96*
St. Rosalia, *53*
Storyville, 20, *54, 82*
Syme-Hardy Family tomb, *39*

Temple Sinai Congregation, 60
The Perfect Union Lodge 1 tomb, *68*
Thevis, Fr. Peter, 90
Third Order of St. Francis, 95
Tombs
  communal tombs, ix, *32, 70*
  design of, ix
  entombment ordinance, 13
  in-ground burials, 60, *61*, 66
  oldest, viii
  types of, 102
  (*See also particular tombs and plots in this index*)

Touro, Judah, 42
Touro Synagogue, 60
Tujague Family, 55

Vampire. *See* Lestat (vampire)
Vampire tomb, *34*
Villere, Jacques Philippe, viii, *28*
Voltaire, 66
Vonderbank, Babette. *See* Ahrens, Babette Vonderbank
Voodoo, *12*
Voodoo Queen. *See* Laveau, Marie ("Voodoo Queen")

Wall vaults, *22-23*
Walton, James B., *87*
Washington, George, 66
Washington Artillery, Louisiana Branch monument, *87*
Weiblen, Albert, *77*
Weldon, Felix de, *83*
Williams, Nellie (dedication), 5

Yellow fever, 13, *18,* 20, *26*, 27, *27,* 30, *31*, 48, 54, 90, *92*, 103
You, Dominique, *22*

About the Author...

Jennie N. Robinson, APRN, has been writing since she was a teenager, beginning with poetry. A resident of the New Orleans area, her career in the healthcare industry began as a hospice worker. Today, she is a nurse practitioner engaged in family medicine. She continues to write poetry and is fascinated by the history of New Orleans that is reflected in its cemeteries.

About the Photographer...

Carl D. Robinson, M.D., is a semi-retired pediatrician and describes himself as a semi-professional photographer. A resident of the New Orleans area, he has been active in photography since 2004, continuously upgrading his skills through workshops, seminars and lots of practice. He enjoys recording scenes in nature, landscapes and – one of his favorite subjects – New Orleans cemeteries.

Intriguing Books About Historic New Orleans

From Bags to Riches
How the New Orleans Saints and the people of their hometown rose from the depths together

The inspiring story of the New Orleans Saints' 2009-2010 football season that culminated with the winning of the Super Bowl. The book explains how the struggling NFL team and the storm-weary people of New Orleans and the Gulf Coast lifted one another's spirits – and fortunes – in the post-Hurricane Katrina years, 2006 – 2010. The narrative is a study in contrasting moods, ranging from the depression and despair that come with being victims of the worst natural disaster in U.S. history, to the euphoria that accompanies the winning of the Super Bowl after 43 years of mostly losing seasons. (Author: Jeff Duncan ISBN: 0-925417-68-8. Price: $24.95)

The Terrible Storms of 2005
Hurricane Katrina and Hurricane Rita

A 184-page book about the 2 devastating hurricanes that struck Louisiana in 2005 – and the heroic efforts of many to rescue victims of the storms. Katrina was "the worst natural disaster in U.S. history," leaving New Orleans severely flooded and more than 1,800 people dead. Rita leveled Cameron, La., and led to the deaths of dozens of evacuees fleeing the storm in nearby southeast Texas. Illustrated with 32 pages of color photos, plus maps. The book also features a special section on pet rescues. (Editor: Trent Angers. Hardcover ISBN: 0-925417-94-7. Price: $17.95.)

An Airboat on the Streets of New Orleans
A Cajun couple lends a hand after Hurricane Katrina floods the city

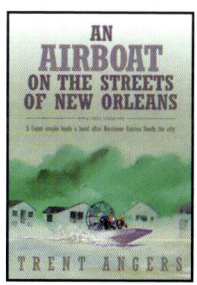

A 192-page book about a Cajun couple from Breaux Bridge, La., who took their airboat into New Orleans when the city flooded as a result of Hurricane Katrina. Doug Bienvenu, the airboat operator, and Drue LeBlanc, who was suffering with kidney disease, rescued hundreds of people during their 3-day mission of mercy. (Author: Trent Angers. Hardcover ISBN: 0-925417-87-4. Price: $16.95. Softcover ISBN: 0-925417-88-2. Price: $14.95.)

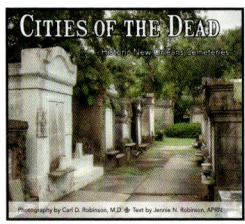

Cities of the Dead
Historic New Orleans Cemeteries

A 112-page hardcover pictorial, in handy 7 x 6 format, with 101 color photos of above-ground graves and monuments in 11 New Orleans cemeteries. Brief texts describe the history and distinguishing characteristics of each cemetery. Complete with index, map locating the featured cemeteries, and timeline of significant dates in New Orleans history. (Author, Jennie Robinson; Photographer, Dr. Carl Robinson. ISBN: 0-9995884-0-0. Price $15.95.)

Blessed Be Jazz
The Story of My Life as a Clarinet-Playing Jesuit Priest in the French Quarter of New Orleans

The 192-page hardcover autobiography of Rev. Frank Coco, SJ (1920-2006), a Jesuit priest who served for more than 50 years in south Louisiana as a retreat director, high school teacher and jazz musician. Using his clarinet, he performed extensively in New Orleans nightclubs, sitting in with some of the best-known jazz musicians of his time, including Ronnie Kole, Al Hirt and Pete Fountain. (Author: Rev. Frank Coco, SJ. ISBN: 0-925417-89-0. Price: $19.95)

Southern Jesuit Biographies

A 256-page hardcover book containing brief biographies of 220 Jesuit priests and brothers who served the people of the Southeastern and Southwestern U.S. Spanning a period of some 300 years, their work included teaching in schools and colleges, preaching the Gospel, building churches and schools, administering the sacraments, leading retreats, working with the poor, and promoting peace and justice. The book is well-illustrated with photographs, both historic and contemporary, as well as maps. (Authors: Rev. Jerome Neyrey, S.J., and Rev. Thomas Clancy, S.J. ISBN: 0-925417-92-0. Price: $40.00)

The Top 100 NEW ORLEANS Recipes of All Time

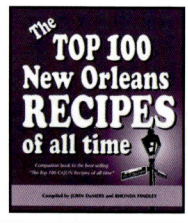

A best-selling cookbook containing 100 of the recipes that have helped to make New Orleans food world-famous. For example, Shrimp Creole, Red Beans & Rice, Blackened Redfish, Oyster Loaf, Muffaletta, Beignets, Café au Lait and King Cake. (Hardcover ISBN: 0-925417-51-3. Price $16.95. Softcover ISBN: 0-925417-84-X. Price $8.95)

TO ORDER, list the books you wish to purchase along with the corresponding cost of each. For shipping & handling, add $4 for the first book and $1 for each additional book thereafter. Louisiana residents add 9% tax to the cost of the books. Mail your order and check or credit card authorization (VISA/MC/AmEx) to: Acadian House Publishing, Dept. COTD, P.O. Box 52247, Lafayette, LA 70505. Or call (800) 850-8851. To order online, go to www.acadianhouse.com.